Liturgy Needs Community
Needs Liturgy

Liturgy
Needs Community
Needs Liturgy

The Possibilities for Parish Liturgy

by
Gabe Huck

PAULIST PRESS
New York/ Paramus / Toronto

Library of Congress
Catalog Card Number: 73-84360

ISBN 0-8091-1791-6

Designed by Morris Berman

Published by Paulist Press
Editorial Office: 1865 Broadway, N.Y., N.Y. 10023
Business Office: 400 Sette Drive, Paramus, N.J. 07652

Printed and bound in the
United States of America

ACKNOWLEDGEMENTS

Dietrich Bonhoeffer, *Letters and Papers From Prison*. New York,
Macmillan, London, SCM Press, Copyright © 1967, 1971. Used with
permission.

Dietrich Bonhoeffer, *Life Together*. New York, Harper & Row,
1954. Used with permission.

Ernst Fuchs, *Studies of the Historical Jesus*. London, SCM Press.
Used with permission.

Robert Funk, *Language, Hermeneutic, and the Word of God*. New
York, Harper & Row, 1966. Used with permission.

Paul W. Hoon, *Integrity of Worship*. Nashville, Abingdon Press,
1971. Used with permission.

Robert W. Hovda in *Living Worship,* December, 1971. Washington, The Liturgical Conference, 1971. Used with permission.

Remy Kwant, *The Phenomenology of Expression.* Translated by Henry J. Koren. Pittsburgh, Duquesne University Press, 1969. Used with permission.

Eta Linneman, *Jesus of the Parables.* New York, Harper & Row, 1966. Used with permission.

William Alexander Percy, "They Cast Their Nets in Galilee". Original copyright by William Alexander Percy and Yale University Press. Used with the permission of LeRoy Pratt Percy.

Gerardus Van Der Leeuw, *Religion in Essence and Development.* Gloucester, Massachusetts, Peter Smith. Used with permission.

Joachim Wach, *The Sociology of Religion.* Urbana, Illinois, University of Illinois Press, 1944. Used with permission.

Amos N. Wilder, *Early Christian Rhetoric.* Cambridge, Massachusetts, Harvard University Press, 1971. Used with permission.

Gibson Winter, *The New Creation as Metropolis.* New York, Macmillan, Copyright © Gibson Winter, 1963. Used with permission.

Contents

Contents

Introduction

This book is for congregations serious about good liturgy. It speaks largely from and to a Roman Catholic experience, but many other churches, especially those with strong liturgical traditions, will find much that sounds familiar. Though the size of the parish, whether it is urban or suburban or rural, and other factors enter into the thinking behind any particular liturgical celebration, these variables will not influence the content of our discussion: it should be equally useful to all.

This is a book about why liturgies are good or bad, effective or ineffective, boring or moving. It is about the nature of the beast we are working with. It is addressed to the situation that so many parishes are in: the reforms of recent years having demonstrated with a painful clarity that liturgies are not made in Rome or the conference rooms of bishops, nor are they made effective by the addition of two guitars and a banner.

Parishes have now accepted mediocrity or have begun the time- and energy-consuming local work of liturgy planning. At this stage, the planners are most likely to turn to one of a number of aids that exist: there are collections of recently created texts like Gallen's *Eucharistic Liturgies* (Paulist), or Hoey's *The Experimental Liturgy Book* (Herder) or The Free Church of Berkeley's *Liberation Prayer Book* (Morehouse-

Barlow); there are dozens of records of new religious folk songs of immensely varied quality; there are overall approaches to the work of the committee like the Liturgical Conference's *Liturgy Committee Handbook*.

Here we want to be a little more fundamental so that we can be a lot more practical. Many parishes have used the above-mentioned tools and others like them to great advantage. Others have created their own resources. Many, many more have yet to get into the struggle at all. But in all cases, what seems most lacking is a feeling for what it is that we want to do with a liturgy, for what kind of a thing liturgy is. Our approach has too often been to omit this step. Consequently we are like someone trying to fix an automobile with the repair manual from a refrigerator. We have not taken the trouble to find out what makes liturgies tick.

That is not to say that liturgy is a matter of finding the right formulas. Anyone who has had experiences of bad liturgy (that's all of us) and good liturgy (most of us, but not too often) know that. But neither is it totally mysterious. It is a human creation. Understanding it is like learning to use the tools of any craft or art; such understanding does not make one a craftsman or an artist, but lack of it keeps one from creating.

We are not seeking to open up the chicken and egg question of liturgy and community: Do you first have good liturgy to create a community or do real communities get themselves together before they get liturgies together? We'll say simply, both. Or neither. Hopefully, after we've discussed it, that will seem like the wrong set of questions.

Though much of what is said would be applicable to intentional communities which celebrate liturgies, the primary focus is the average congregation. It is in that structure that most Christians celebrate what may be their only experience of religious ritual; it is there that most of the hard work of planning liturgies is now beginning. So the "community" of the title means whatever that congregation is now and can become in the possible future.

Our starting point is ritual itself. There is no worthy Christian liturgy apart from simple, good ritual. Most often we have failed to appreciate that. Theologians have failed, reformers have failed, liturgy committees have had little choice but to fail. Christians should have been applying their notion of the incarnation: it's all natural, first. After we understand ritual we can speak of what it means to design liturgies, where the Christian community experiences ritual and is affected by it. Finally, we will want to deal with the content of Christian liturgical expression.

Whether this book is read by an individual or used by any groups planning liturgies, it should generate practical thinking about the creating of effective ritual, whether in the family or the congregation. Thus, take it a chapter at a time and make use of the occasional practical suggestions as at least mental exercises that will accustom you to thinking concretely about ritual and its potential.

1. Holding the
pennant high and
shaking hands

On September 30, 1971 the Washington Senators, after 71 years, played their last baseball game in Washington. The owner was moving the team to Dallas and the fans were angry with him. That last game was the most vivid proof I've ever had that we of the 1970's need ritual as much as and can create it as well as the people of the 1370's or the 670's or the 1970's B.C.

There was the visual dimension. About 20,000 people were there and the loudspeakers were, of course, controlled by the establishment. Not a word could be said over them to protest the move; nor could anything be flashed on the scoreboard. The anger toward the owner and the feelings of gratitude and sad leave-taking toward the players would have to be expressed without electronics in a gigantic stadium (which, even on this occasion, was less than half full). The fans, young ones mostly, used a variety of banners, signs, posters. Some were vertical, hung from the third tier for the enjoyment of those across the field. Others were written, one letter or word to a poster, and carried by the creators in the proper order, parading from one level to another.

But more was involved than the medium. There was first of all the thought that had gone into deciding what to say: how, in the fewest possible words, to express the sentiment most strongly. Then the creation of the sign: contrasting colors, so that it could be read from a distance and would have some kind of attraction about it. The choice of words took on another dimension since space was limited if the words were to be large, and since the police would be seizing those they considered obscene. Timing had to be considered: all of the displays were not in place when the first pitch was thrown. Rather, they appeared throughout the game, not so much competing with the game for attention as placing it within the proper, and larger, context. When the police decided a sign was too strong and had to be hauled up or torn down there was the added element of a miniature good guys vs. bad guys test of strength: fans booing the police and cheering the bold sign-makers as the sign was being destroyed and its makers ejected from the game.

The Senators had but one player that year who even approached star or hero status, a status built on his hitting. In the fifth inning he hit what may well have been one of the few ritual homeruns in the history of baseball; the fans went crazy. The pitcher and coach of the opposing team never denied that a deliberately easy pitch was thrown, and the Senator hero didn't seem to mind their generosity, if that is what it was. For the fans, it was the last of the many exciting moments this man had provided them, moments for which they had good reason to be grateful since the team had, over the years, managed an almost permanent lease on last place. The cheering went on long after their hero had reentered the dugout. He had never been known to give any special acknowledgement to this kind of demonstration. But it went on and on. Finally he stepped out for a moment and waved as if he hoped that would end it. It didn't. A full minute or more later, he appeared again and tossed his hat into the stands. Finally, the noise began to lessen and the game continued.

The final, most perfect, ritual happened as the

Senators took the field in the top of the eighth inning. Play was almost to begin when, noticed first by a few and then by most and soon by everyone in the park, a young man came dashing from behind the first base dugout toward the first baseman. In his left hand he held a pennant like the colors' bearer in the old westerns used to hold the flag. His right hand was held out. He reached the first baseman (who was our homerun hitting hero), shook his hand hard, and the cheering began to mount. By this time two policemen were running after him. When the crowd saw this, and saw too that the young man had no intention of turning around, but was headed instead for the second baseman, then the shortstop, there was wild applause, whistling, cheering; not a person was sitting down. Police were waiting for him on the other side of the third baseman, but he made an end run and fans reached down to pull him back into the stands.

That game taught me as much about ritual as any liturgy I have ever attended. The planned and the spontaneous, the natural and the role-playing, timing, color, sound, poetry, gesture, movement—every element was there. Here were 20,000 people with little in common except anger for a man who had abused them and sorrow at saying good-bye to some old friends and small-time celebrities they would never see again. This brought them out there. But strong feelings require more than physical presence if they are to work themselves out. If 20,000 individuals were to be more than that, someone had to find the signs with which everyone there could identify: a few words, an easy pitch, a hat, and most of all a well-timed handshake.

It is difficult for us to begin thinking about ritual

action and liturgy planning in this context. We may
have thought of ritual as something that applies to
nonreligious dimensions of life, but we have seldom
thought about whether or not the factors that govern
good ritual at a baseball game are the same as those
that determine good ritual around the altar. Since the
people are the same (or rather, for the same people) the
forms of good ritual must be the same.

The committee that sits down to plan Sunday mass
should take a break every so often to fantasize about
the kind of ritual they would plan for a ballgame like
that described above if it happened in their town; or for
the civic celebration of Memorial Day; or for the end of
a day of tree planting. What are four things at least
some people in the community have strong feelings
about and how could these be ritualized (put aside the
question of whether or not these feelings agree with
your own moral sense)? Think practically.

You will learn first that you are working with
signs. We know this about our liturgy, but we can be so
accustomed to the repetition and carelessness that the
signs are dulled in their effect on us. We work with
signs because ritual comes into play when we want to
go beyond words, when we have something to express,
to celebrate, to share that cannot be done in the prose
of everyday life.

We make a ritual or we adapt a ritual or we do
again a familiar ritual. We get into signmaking because
signs speak to more than the mind; the good sign involves our whole self. The sign is the thing that brings
the full meaning of the moment to bear on us. It may
be taps or the placing of the folded flag on a mother's
lap at her son's military funeral; it may be the steps a

child takes in first crossing a street alone; it may be the flower pressed in some seldom opened book; it may be notes of music a couple can identify as "our song." It is signs that matter.

When we put these kinds of things into words at all, we call those words poetry. When we wish to deal wholly with anything, great or trivial, we are wise to ban prose as much as possible and to deal with our deep feelings and beliefs and hopes only in signs.

What signs have spoken to you most deeply in the past year?
In your whole life?
What made them so strong and memorable and right?
List some characteristics of these events; think in terms of time and timing, of movement, of sounds and silences.
How was feeling shared, intensified, satisfied?
What was the effect on you?
Could anything else have had this same effect?

Where does this take us in regard to the Sunday liturgy of the church? Most importantly, it should help us to use the right tools for the planning of liturgies and the evaluating of them. People who come to Sunday liturgy may not have the same emotional intensity as those attending the last Senators' game, but they do share something. Do they recognize what it is and that they have come to celebrate it with others of like mind and feelings? Many do, but not all, and with good reason.

Certainly, not all are ready to celebrate in the same way, but this should neither surprise nor daunt the liturgy planners. The challenge is to let the ritual of that place and day draw these people into an experience of their shared belief that both invites their involvement and is as involving as each will allow it to be.

The principles and tools for this work (we are not talking now about content) are the same as those that night in Washington's Kennedy Stadium or in those events you remembered from your own life a few moments ago. So what happens to these elements on Sunday morning? We need to look at the elements themselves first, then at the care, planning and style with which they are used.

The general structure of the Roman Rite has endured in so many settings for so long not only because it has had the force of law but because it had the potential of good liturgy. But even in its latest, cleaned-up editions, one problem is with the detail. There is an entrance rite and greeting, a penitential rite, possibly the Gloria, and the prayer of the day: all introductory matter (after song rehearsal and the friendly ushers have already provided their introduction). Then a service of the word that is fairly simple but does not explicitly leave room for creativity except in the homily. Then, often, the Creed and the prayer of the faithful. The offertory remains a rather unclear moment, though the eucharistic prayer and the communion and conclusion, in structure at least, are somewhat less burdened with the important and unimportant placed side by side.

Often what will be most strong in a ritual the length of the eucharistic liturgy will take only a few moments. But the work begins with making general decisions about the whole so that when one or more elements on a given Sunday do turn out extraordinarily

High Involvement	Low Involvement
Entrance Song	
Parts of the Service	
Recessional	

well, they are not spoiled by the mediocrity of all else.

The creation of strong liturgical forms for a parish begins with a thorough knowledge of the general format *as ritual*. It will not work as anything else (even mortification), and should not, if it is not good ritual. The temptation is to make the liturgy less boring by looking only at the songs, or the sermon, or by introducing one or two snappy elements here and there; important as these are, they should not substitute for the establishment of a basic form for the entire eucharistic celebration, which deals with overall structure.

If the celebration is to be effective *as a whole,* then the flow of the whole must be studied and decisions made about the location of songs, movement, parts that are new to each Sunday, silence and song, involvement and noninvolvement of the congregation.

Often it will help to see a diagram of the ritual. Place "high involvement" (hard to let the mind wander is a minimum definition) on the left-hand side of the page at the top and "low involvement" on the right-hand side of the page, also at the top. Then list the parts of the service to one side, in the order they come in the service with the entrance song at the top and the recessional at the bottom. Now rate each of the parts and place an "x" somewhere between high and low involvement. Finally, connect the points and you will be able to visualize something of the flow of the liturgy. (This idea was suggested by John Harrell of Berkeley, California in an article in the February 1970 issue of *Liturgy* magazine.)

Good ritual does not try to maintain high involvement for any length of time, or to connect two or three or more high involvement items together. It is based on

Loud

Soft

a good flow between the two points, and both are necessary. Listening is usually low involvement, singing rather high. But any group attempting this knows what the highs (if there are any) and lows of their community are, Sunday after Sunday. Perhaps the flow is there. Or perhaps the flow isn't there: between the entrance song and communion there's a straight line down the right hand of the page. In either case, the problem has been identified.

The next step is study of the parts, deciding which to emphasize, which to change, which to eliminate, which to make unique each Sunday, which to make similar and familiar each Sunday. You may decide, for example, that the acclamation during the eucharistic prayer is tremendously important to the flow of good ritual, that it must always be sung or shouted, that a variety of forms must be developed and used at nearly every Sunday service. Or you may decide that the peace greeting right before communion links two high involvement items (but is the communion really that?) too closely and that the peace greeting should come as part of the confession at the beginning of the service.

Obviously, parts are not rearranged only on the basis of involvement; there must be respect for the integrity of the whole and the significance of each part.

A similar graph can be done with "loud" and "soft" as the two sides, for here also there should be a flow, with ample consideration of the importance of complete silence, or silence with music in the background.

Another chart could be done in a somewhat similar manner to show the flow of the movement and gestures of the ministers or the movement of the whole

Movement and Gestures of the Ministers	**Movement of the whole congregation**

congregation. Naturally, the questions that one then puts to such a chart change with the object under consideration. In all, we try to get some idea of the qualities and potential of the ritual activity we are working with.

Sometimes it is necessary for those involved in the creation of better liturgies to free themselves a bit from the mental restrictions we can all place on this sort of work. One professor of homiletics was told to loosen his seminarians up, make them feel at home in the ritual situation.

Rather than put them to work within the context of the eucharistic liturgy, where they would have all kinds of presuppositions and conditioned reflexes, he asked them to create a raindance, something from a different age and culture. (See "Paperwads and a Raindance" by Severin Foley, *Liturgy,* July 1972.) He divided the class into committees to plan the dance, with each committee responsible for one part of a five part service: 1. Getting the attention of the rain god. 2. Informing the possibly stupid rain god of the people's needs. 3. Presenting the rain god with various gifts as inducement for him to send rain. 4. Threats to transfer affections to rival gods should rain not come. 5. Exit procession (presumably in the rain).

The point of such an exercise is not only to sharpen the skills that are equally at use in raindance or mass (both planning and celebrating skills), but to see these kinds of ritual actions in a setting that we will not take seriously. (I am not sure what to do about the question: Are there any peoples with raindance committees to spark up dull raindances who would be helped by doing an exercise that involved planning, say, the Christmas midnight mass? And if not, why not?) If a group takes their task seriously enough and themselves lightly enough to get into this kind of exercise, they should by all means carry it through and do the dance. Musicians, assistants and celebrant should take their accustomed roles. Make sure the dance conforms to the standards you have set for the liturgy in terms of the flow of involvement, sound, movement, etc.

The dance, like the baseball game, illustrates how much of ritual involves the body beyond the vocal chords. Dance is more basic to the religious rituals of the world than anything else (one can almost imagine our raindance committee getting into the question of the need for "nonbodily" elements as we get into the need for "nonverbal" elements).

At the ballgame many of the ritual actions were physical gestures (the homerun pitch, the thrown hat, the run and handshake) as were the ritual responses (the cheering, applauding, stomping, whistling, jumping). Yet no one comes to church expecting to be asked to use ritual that involves movement other than standing, sitting and kneeling, walking up to communion and perhaps a peace greeting. We have created a physical setup, pews, that just about guarantees we won't ask people to do anything beyond this. While many signs in the society point to at least a recognition of the importance of people getting in touch with their bodies, our basic liturgical structures provide for this less now than they did before the changes (when breast beating, cross making, double genuflections and folded hands were common).

This point is raised at the beginning because it needs to be kept in mind throughout all parts of liturgy planning. The basic outline for a parish's Sunday services should not be considered complete until ways of incorporating certain gestures and movements as more or less constant parts of the service have been decided on, at least for a period of experimentation. The advantages of smaller congregations and pewless rooms are obvious. But there are possibilities in anything less than a crowded cathedral. An extremely helpful book on this subject is Joe Wise's *The Body at Liturgy* published by North American Liturgy Resources.

Good ritual action has other qualities beyond the kinds of rhythm we have discussed. Rituals are to be celebrated with great care. We have for too long been sloppy celebrators, perhaps because we were so influenced by a notion that it wasn't *how* it was done so much as *that* it was done that mattered.

One example we are all familiar with. In the early months of 1971 the Federation of Diocesan Liturgy Commissions began to make unhappy noises about the multiplication of missalettes. Their proposal was modest enough: that the publishers eliminate the texts of the readings and the eucharistic prayers so that, at least during these parts, the people would have to listen and the readers and celebrants would have to do well. There are many other good reasons, however, for doing away with the missalettes. Primarily: they almost of themselves create a careless, sloppy liturgy.

I once had a professor who had mimeographed copies of his lectures. He would pass these out to the students before the class, take a copy for himself and read to us for an hour. It was difficult to know whether to be just bored or really insulted. Many quit coming and few of those who came ever bothered to listen. By the third class meeting our professor could have been delivering an entirely different lecture.

Nothing characterizes our indifference to good liturgy like the missalette. No one demands a script when going to a play or musical, no one wants the transcript of *Firing Line* or *Meet the Press* before it goes on so that the whole can be followed word for word. Despite the reasoning and despite the jokes (Jesus, in a Da Vinci Last Supper setting, saying: "We'll use eucharistic prayer three and acclamation 'C.' ") the business grows, meeting the worshipping public's demand for poor liturgy.

When a parish is careful of its liturgy, there is no need or demand for missalettes because ritual is not something to be "followed along" but something to do, all of it. That care shows itself in the quality of the reading, the hospitality of the building and the people, the clarity and beauty with which a theme is developed, the relation and understanding between all those responsible for various parts of the service.

Another overall quality of good ritual is style. This pertains to the various persons who take leadership roles, and especially to the celebrant. Most celebrants were trained when celebrating mass was a matter of learning a sequence of words and gestures, more or less invariable, without much significance in themselves. Training today is entirely different. The celebrant understands that his (soon, his or her) presence is not a neutral force, but either adds to or detracts from the overall quality of the celebration. He learns that his is one role among many, but, as the speaker of the eucharistic prayer, is the most important.

Gestures, words, eyes, all must be studied, must be

seen through the eyes of others and through his own eyes so that things do not happen by accident. Celebrants may bring lesser or greater gifts for the task they are to do, but there is much that can be learned. All involved need to overcome any conscious or unconscious disdain for the skills of the performer.

Learning to perform well, whether it be the celebrant doing the eucharistic prayer or the song leader doing the verses of a psalm, is essential to good liturgy. A thick skin and a willingness to change one's ways are practically prerequisites for all who would take leadership roles in the assembly. Criticism must be freely asked and freely given. We are newly come to the work of good ritual and can learn a little from everyone.

It may seem by now that we are making liturgy a very human thing with little room left for the presence of God. Yet God, now as always, is finding and surprising us through each other and especially through our efforts to discover the strongest possible signs for our faith. That is why the task of liturgy is worth undertaking at all. That is why it is vital that we understand the nature of ritual, the same at ballpark and basilica. That is why the ritual is to be a thing of great care, demanding our time and energy and even our money.

A most helpful definition of ritual of this kind is provided by Robert W. Hovda. "Ritual is the intense and concentrated expression of the purpose and meaning we believe but cannot put into words." (*Living Worship,* December 1971.) Without robbing this of its simplicity, we might briefly examine some of the notions involved.

The first of these is that of "concentrated expression." It might be helpful for readers to construct their own list of the various forms such signs take in the eucharistic liturgy alone: bread and wine, tangible, visible, perhaps even able-to-be-tasted-and-smelled objects; the gospel book, also an object; standing, kneeling, sitting, all bodily signs; the Creed, a symbolic saying of what it means to be a Christian. And many more. Perhaps too many for all to be effective, even when they are treated reverently.

Intensity of the signs means that they are not simply a kind of shorthand, not a way of saying quickly what otherwise would take too long. They are rather ways of saying with signs what cannot be said in any other way because it is said not simply to the mind of man but to body, soul, spirit.

As such, signs are terribly dependent on those who make them, for they involve human creativity and talent in their every aspect. To cite a couple of examples from the eucharistic liturgy. The bread and wine cannot be signs unless they first are, and appear to as many senses as possible to be, real bread and real wine. But this sign takes its power not only from shape, color, smell and taste, but also from the manner in which it is handled, the dish and the cup, the gestures which embrace them, offer them, share them.

The way these things are done strongly influences the meaning which the sign has. For example: bread placed in the hand, with the hands of the two persons touching for a moment, conveys one set of meanings about the ritual. But bread placed directly into the mouth of another conveys another set of meanings. It is not a matter of one set being right, the other wrong, but of the kind of sign we wish to make. Both may be faithful to the overall meaning of the celebration, but that does not mean our decision can be lightly taken. We deal with a particular time and place and people and must, with these people, seek the best possible sign.

Many signs have taken a beating in recent years as people reacted to the stiffness of the Roman Rite. Informal celebrations of the eucharist sometimes did away with signs altogether in an effort to let people "be themselves." Most have learned by now that only with signs can that happen. The "doughnuts and coke" eucharists came and went because people were able to honestly admit that something was missing. The eucharist is not just another friendly meal but a serious effort by persons to express what they mean and believe.

"Expression . . . of . . . what cannot be put into words" is a notion we will be talking about later, but it must be understood here that this is a kind of communication which most often takes us into the realm of art. And that is enough to make most of us feel uneasy, for we exist in a culture that separates art and the artist from "normal" existence and gives little chance for each individual to develop the artistic abilities that are within. *Things* dominate our culture, and not beautiful things, but disposable, mass-produced things. We are to consume these things, be they paper napkins or national parks.

We are ill-prepared to move into the realm of the spirit, ill-prepared to be believers in the kingdom of God for such a belief can be kept alive only by constant renewal through experiencing and expressing the signs of that kingdom in powerful ways: poetry, song, dance, color and shape. Anyone who deals with ritual, in the family or the congregation, must come to terms with how hard these things come in our culture yet how vital they are to the building up of the church or any other community.

We know well enough what it is when the signs in liturgy are not allowed to make themselves clear. We know what it is to have paper-like wafers substituted for bread, to have signs of the cross raced through, to have words mumbled and mixed, to have celebrants without understanding of the humanness of ritual. Yet even here the lights and colors and gestures and unclear words could create a sense of mystery and belonging. How much more possible is that sense when ritual is used well!

How far would Hitler have gotten without "Sieg Heil" and the stiff-armed salute? Where would Mao be without the Little Red Book? Would the "movement" in the United States have felt nearly so strong in the late sixties without the flashed "V"? Or would anything much have happened on the race problem of the United States between 1966 and 1968 if Stokely Carmichael hadn't shouted "Black Power!" one day in Mississippi? It is with rituals that movements and communities grow and hand on what it is that they mean and believe. These nonrational signs concentrate into a gesture, a phrase, an object, a set of meanings that become a kind of home for the believer. Think of the forces that have shaped our country, from the Pilgrims to the colonists-in-revolt to the K.K.K. to Billy Graham to Zero Population Growth. Make your own list and by each force list the kinds of rituals or signs that are associated with it.

But when it comes to our parish communities, what signs do we have to list? What are the rituals through which we identify with one another? For many older Catholics, these are definately present: the rosary (as a symbolic object and as a prayer), certain devotions and prayers, stations of the cross. They are things of the church building and things of the home. But they have not been assimilated by younger generations, just as the symbols of the older generations of union people have not been taken up by the younger, and there are probably parallels in the military, the schools, etc.

List your own forces and associated signs (see next page).

Forces	Associated Signs

**2.
What do
we have
to celebrate?**

So many parents are left today asking not only how they are to communicate faith to their children, but what is this faith they are to hand on. What gives the gathering of Christians they see on Sunday its distinction from any other gathering of Christians, or non-Christians for that matter?

For a long time the communication has been entrusted to parochial schools and Sunday schools where emphasis was on doctrine; recent years have seen more of a move toward the emphasis on values, but the effects have not been terribly tangible. Throughout, there has been little effort *to seek new or revitalize old signs* of the faith in church, school or home. The home, in fact, enters in only as the place where the decision is made about whether or not the child is to have religious training, and if so whether it is to be parochial school or Sunday school. Efforts to involve parents in the religious formation programs have been limited mainly to sacramental preparation.

The signs of our faith, like most else, have been treated as things to be learned about. We teach that the fish is or was a symbol because the first letters of "Jesus Christ, Son of God, Savior," in the Greek language, spell "fish." But we do not use the fish as a sign, a way of identifying one another. We learn various interpretations of what happens with the bread and wine in the eucharistic liturgy, but we do not learn to make and do a celebration of that liturgy.

Nowhere, except in the church building itself, do we have signs, rituals, that we can use without embarrassment or uneasiness, and, if we do these in church they are most often done poorly and can be done at all only because we have conditioned ourselves to separation of church ceremony from the realities of everyday life. In no way is it becoming that kind of ritual life which defines a community of meaning and belief, strengthens it, gives it identity and continuity.

Our greatest assets here may be a rich tradition to draw on, an awakening sense of imagination, and the very feeling of need. The latter is today not verbalized only in terms of children, but in terms of the adults themselves. And that is necessary for we will have something to offer our children only when we have built communities that fulfill our own needs. I doubt that there is much hope for the rediscovery of strong community-created and -creating rituals on the parish level until this begins to happen on the family level.

Here we may be able to learn much from Jewish families. It would seem that so much of their process of growth and communication is through ritual within the family. This is not to say that synagogue worship and the study of the scriptures and other writings are unimportant in the formation process. But the basic work is done in what would seem, if we had not taken such an entirely different track, the most natural setting of all, the family.

Passover, for example, is a family feast kept with a ritual that involves weeks of preparation before the seder itself. In this way one feels a part not only of a family where tasks, meals and songs and stories are shared, but of a people that extends in both time and place. The foods are rituals for they come once a year, are specially prepared, are common in all the homes, are blessed and passed in given ways, have stories told about them. There are songs that are equally delightful to child and adult and, when the whole thing might become too burdensome to the child, games that are as much a part of the ritual as the unleavened bread itself. There is something else here also that we can easily miss: Passover is kept in a unique way, but so is every other great feast. Each has its traditions, its own kind of anticipation, its own rituals. It is not a matter so much of being able in this way to instruct about many things (our tendency is to see even ritual in terms of catechesis), but of a wealth of imagination at work on a tradition which thus continues to have meaning.

By contrast, we are poor in both breadth and depth. When we celebrate something that has to do with our faith we do it in church. And whether it is Christmas or Easter or the start of school or the end of the war, we do it with the eucharist. Recent years have increased our poverty when, instead of enriching the celebration of the sacraments like penance and baptism and developing new rituals to replace those like the rosary that seemed to have lost their meaning, we simply let all those things we thought of as optional fade away.

Once we had blessings for everything from the ships to the fields to the green scapular. Now we've got the mass. And although there is an increasing sense of this poverty, its effect is more often frustration than a burst of creativity. Especially within the Roman church it would seem that those who are frustrated with official restraints on finding more effective rituals in the eucharistic context should turn to the rich tradition of noneucharistic rituals and to a growing feeling throughout society that people want to create more and consume less.

If a small part of the energy that goes into running a school system or other religious education programs could be directed instead to broadening and deepening our rituals, perhaps then we would be forced to face the question of what it is we have to share, grow in, pass on. There is much to be said for teaching about doctrine and values, whether traditionally or experientially or however, but I doubt if there is ever a culture that has recreated and perpetuated itself solely in this way.

Perhaps it is precisely because we have lacked ritual expression for what we profess that that profession has been able to divorce itself so completely from life. Not that rituals guarantee anything, as a reading of Isaiah and the gospels will show. Except this: for Isaiah and for Jesus it was not the rituals that were wrong, but the hypocrisy with which they were observed. No amount of good and creative ritual will do away with the need for prophets. But between the prophets it is the ritual that bears much of the burden for reminding us of who we are, where we have been and where we are called to go now.

We might begin our efforts with the calendar for the rhythm of time is an essential element of a community's ritual. Within each parish community it should be possible for interested persons to create a local calendar. It would certainly be built first on the great seasons of the traditional liturgical year: Advent, Christmas, Lent and Easter. For a given year, each of these would be given a character in keeping with the meaning tradition gives; Advent, for example, might be four weeks for ritualizing the fears and hopes of this community. Within the season the calendar would build the anticipation through parish and family rituals and through the various programs the community would undertake to give flesh to the dimensions of faith they are then celebrating.

Obviously any such effort depends on a simultaneous improvement of the Sunday eucharistic liturgies. No parish that has one man reading from a missalette, "Alleluia, alleluia, alleluia," and three hundred repeating, in the same uninteresting monotone from the same kind of book, "Alleluia, alleluia, alleluia," can expect families to attempt even the simplest ritual in the home.

The calendar would also include the celebrations of the saints and heroes to be honored locally. This would be quite selective because there would have to be time put into working up to and keeping well the ones chosen. From the calendar of the saints and heroes (naturally, women are included) in all fields, perhaps a dozen or so are selected and, from tradition and local creativity, ways are suggested for the celebrating of these days.

If it is a working class parish, the list would include not only Joseph the Worker but people like Joe Hill and Eugene Debs (the point, of course, is not to "canonize" these but to celebrate them as a vital part of what has been a force for good in our world). A parish with a heavy professional population might choose to celebrate Thomas More and Cosmas and Damian and Florence Nightingale and Clarence Darrow.

Any parish should include women who have struggled to liberate themselves and others, and any United States parish should include those who have forced both black and white to come to terms with racism.

In ways like these we learn where we have been. This can be done from textbooks and biographies (and certainly the telling of the stories is an important part of any such ritual), but they become so much more a part of us when we find signs for joining them to us. There is, of course, nothing new about this even if all we have left is Patrick and his shamrock. Which should remind us that such celebrations of saints and heroes are ways of building respect for the ethnic culture that manages to survive yet in many areas of our country.

In 1972 the Liturgical Conference published a calendar that attempted to stimulate this kind of thinking and activity. It contained far more than any one community would ever want, but its purpose was simply to give a sense of the possibilities. A few excerpts of the suggestions given there might help to show the kind of ritualizing that could take place.

January 1. New Year's Day. A day when all tradition calls for visiting friends and being visited by them. Take lots of last night's nuts (sign of the fruit of the old year and promise of the new) along and include on the rounds friends of each member of the family. "Friendship," says Emerson, "should be surrounded with ceremonies and respects, and not crushed into corners."

January 5. George Washington Carver, 1943, who gave us peanut butter (and much more, but that alone would have been enough). A day to enjoy peanuts and sweet potatoes and to celebrate Twelfth-night.

January 7. 1896—Fannie Farmer, the mother of level measurement, publishes her first cookbook. Obviously, a day to try a new recipe.

June 29. Peter and Paul, Apostles. A day for fishing

and a fish fry (like Peter) or for writing letters, good honest ones (like Paul).

July 24. 1904—Invention of the ice cream cone in Saint Louis. Visit your favorite ice cream parlor or make ice cream at home and feast to your heart's delight. Fresh peaches should be available for the home-made ice cream.

August 6. Transfiguration. An early festival of the harvest, a day for a special trip to the garden or the country to see how things are coming, to sample something fresh and juicy, to celebrate the transfiguration of seed and earth and rain into fruits and vegetables.

    Innocents of Hiroshima, 1945. A week to remember the victims of the atomic bombing of Hiroshima and Nagasake; 115,000 were killed, many more than that made to suffer. Sing the spiritual: "Gonna lay down my sword and shield . . ."

September 13. 1971—Attica Prison massacre. "We will live like people or die!" Attica inmate shortly before police killed 42 inmates and hostages. A day for remembering all prisoners and asking what sense prisons make. "Imprisonment is a worse crime than any of those committed by its victims." George Bernard Shaw.

The calendar of a community is to be a living thing. For the most part, a new year brings a return of the same celebrations, the same preparations, the same rituals, but always with the chance that for good reason there will be change, growth, renewal. And always an openness to new celebrations, be they cause for rejoicing or sorrowing. Such a local calendar can include dates that are important only in that community. It would naturally include the public holidays (July 4th, Labor Day, Memorial Day, Washington's Birthday) and offer suggestions for how these might be kept not only with long weekends, but with a sense of their importance. The calendar quoted above offers the following examples:

July 4. Independence Day. Read the Declaration of Independence and decide whether or not you can sign it. Put the copy, signed or not, on the table. Sing together "Yankee Doodle" and "Go Down, Moses." July 4, 1826—Death of Thomas Jefferson, author (at age 33) of the Declaration of Independence. Jefferson: "God forbid we should ever be twenty years without . . . a rebellion." A Day for remembering all the rebellions we have had since 1776 (labor, ethnics, blacks, women, youth, American Indian) and thinking about those that are now incomplete or not even begun.

May 29. Memorial Day. A day to remember those who have died for believing and doing, and those who have been killed because others believed and did. Sing together today: "Where have all the flowers gone, long time passing; . . ."

Another purpose of such a calendar with its effort to create different kinds of celebrations for different kinds of occasions is to help us get a sense of the cycle that has been the basis for most of man's cultural continuity, as well as his way of realizing his unity with nature. Celebrations of the seasons, even in cities, would usually be an important part of a community's calendar.

There is, of course, far more to this than long tradition. We might say that in the face of the heresy of unlimited exploitation of the earth by the few, to the harm of the many and the whole future, the church (precisely as she has done with other kinds of heresies in the past) must institute rituals and celebrations of the truth: that the earth is the Lord's and not the private property of any group of men, that the goods of the earth are meant to move in a cycle, not a straight line that returns nothing to the earth but only takes from her; that man is indeed mortal and needs to be as much at home on the earth as his brothers and sisters, the insects and the animals.

Scholars have conjectured that man's first ritual action may have been a grain of wheat, plucked in silence. Anyone involved or concerned with the renewal of ritual would do well to ponder that.

It would seem that we do have a great deal to celebrate, but that until now we have not tried. If we are willing to do the hard work of finding the rituals that express our feelings and convictions about our faith in Jesus and its meaning for attitudes and decisions of everyday living, then we can expect communities to emerge in a way that they have not yet done in the structures of the parishes.

Within the parish it involves giving liturgy a priority it has not had for a long time. It means making it a focus for all other parish activities, especially any involving Christian education. There is only so much time, so much energy and so much money. Liturgy will not fit as another program beside the many. It has a priority because it is the very reason for the existence of a parish. If done well, it can integrate the other activities.

There are many things that can keep this from happening. One of them is the very understanding we have of the church. For Roman Catholics especially, the church is seen first in terms of the whole church and, while this has certain obvious benefits (which don't seem to pay off when it comes to things like war and hunger), it makes the parish little more than a service station. Pastors and assistants come and go at the will of the bishop and there is a depressing sameness that runs through the vast majority of parishes.

The things that distinguish one from another, aside from personalities of clergy which are here today, gone tomorrow, are terribly insignificant in the light of what one might expect. A group of people whose association is based on their religious faith would seem to have so much tied up in their community that unique forms would be springing up in each special community. But that has not been our experience or expectation.

Nearly 20 years ago Karl Rahner began to offer some thoughts on a new theological position that might lead to practical policies on the part of churches to create new attitudes and experiences. Rahner wrote of the local community not as a mere part of the whole, "but as a visible manifestation of the whole." The event of the eucharist, which is local in nature, is that by which the church continues. The parish, because it is based on one of the main factors of man's society, his at-homeness, is the primary realization of the church as event. Since man has other ways of creating community, the church may realize itself in other forms: work, interest, organizations, language, etc. (*The Parish: From Theology to Practice,* by Karl Rahner, ed. Hugo Rahner, Westminster, Maryland: Newman Press, 1958, pp. 25-29.)

But greater local autonomy alone will not set the stage for an outbreak of creativity in ritual and other activities. The loss of community flows also from the increasing functionless role of the church group, the lack of difference it makes in the lives of people. But what we are talking about here in our discussion of ritual is bringing the local community into contact with every area that does make a difference to people, while at the same time creating the atmosphere where new kinds of priorities (difference-makers) can be suggested. It is not a question of relevance only through church statements on racism, unemployment, the family, property; rather, it is a matter of specific, involving, cyclical celebrations of the events and heroes and occasions that embody the Judeo-Christian belief in the meaning and direction of life.

In some cases parishes are attempting to recreate themselves on a level that is more functional, more human in scale. Maintaining the larger institution for purposes of service, they divide on the basis of geography or interest into smaller groups. It is here that the community rituals should take place with the whole parish coming together only for the greater festivals, two or three times a year.

In the smaller groups responsibilities for many matters that would ordinarily be left to the clergy are placed in the hands of the laity; this would include the planning and celebration of the liturgy. Perhaps the eucharistic celebration in some communities would be held less often than once a week, but the community would gather on other Sundays for morning or evening prayer or the celebration of a festival liturgy of its own creation. In such a setting there could be attention given to the individuals and families, with the development of appropriate rituals and activities for the home as a follow-through to the group's ritual. This type of follow-through would, of course, be equally good when the group's celebration was the eucharist.

Other parishes are attempting to exist on a more human scale by creating a number of communities within themselves through offering a wide variety of styles in the celebrations of the Sunday liturgy. One such parish in the Washington, D.C. area has eleven weekend masses, each different. They have found that each creates its own community.

Most parishes have to date done this only with one folk mass and one sung mass, leaving all else about the liturgies substantially the same. This is the result more of a lack of a sense of the possibilities than of a refusal of the extra energy needed for the creation of a variety of celebrations each Sunday. In a moderate sized parish, this kind of diversity can actually channel the differences between parishioners so that there results a much greater spirit of cooperation when issues arise that confront the whole parish.

Such a program has to be based on a mutual respect on all sides as well as a conviction, by Latin mass fans as well as those who want rock and multi-media, that good liturgical celebrations are the responsibility of the whole worshipping congregation. A parish can welcome the greatest diversity in good celebrations but should not tolerate the mediocre however far-out or far-in the congregation is purported to be. Nor does such a diversity of celebrations imply that there is one gospel preached to one group, another to another. It is the art forms in which ritual takes shape that change, not the content of the ritual. Moreover, there should be some matters on which all groups can cooperate such as the decision about participation aids.

A good formation program for the leadership of each community should establish the undesirability of the monthly missalette (both because of the reprinting of the text and because as a liturgical book all of those now available leave nearly everything to be desired). The question then becomes one of selecting a bound hymnal, loose-leaf hymnal, or using slides or an overhead projector.

In many cases the loose-leaf hymnal will be best since it maintains a traditional form, allows for additional material and can meet the specific needs of each group. Such a hymnal has a high initial cost, especially if, as should be, copyrights are secured for each hymn not in the public domain. Here and in other areas the various worshipping communities within the one parish will need to work together on a budget realizing that the needs of some groups may be more costly than those of others. They may want to opt for each group raising its own liturgy budget, but this can cause more problems than it solves.

More cooperation will be needed on deciding the arrangement of the worship space itself. Since there will ordinarily not be a great deal of time between celebrations (though it is well to allow for the maximum here) groups must either agree on whatever visuals are to be introduced (such as banners, altar decorations, etc.) on a given Sunday, or each must take care to leave the space as it was found.

An increasing number of churches are being built or remodeled using folding or stacking chairs instead of pews. Besides allowing the room to be used for other purposes, chairs allow for the space to be created differently when the liturgy calls for this. Also, only as many chairs need be used as there are people so that the usual effect of pews, scattering and separation, is avoided.

A parish that is without pews and considering a diversified liturgy program may want to investigate the use of space dividers, especially if it is likely that the groups will vary greatly in size and that some of them will be experimenting with a variety of art forms. Treehouse Productions of Dayton, Ohio is producing attractive, lightweight dividers made of canvas and steel tubing that are ideal for this purpose. Each three-fold panel is 5' high and 7½' long and weighs only 25 lbs. They are designed so that they may be used with various easily made strips of butcher paper (and paint, collage, or whatever) to create an environment suitable to the theme of the liturgy. For example, at a baptismal liturgy the congregation may be surrounded by the panels, all covered with the white paper, with wide blue flowing lines painted on the bottom half all the way around. In contrast to most space dividers, because of their light weight, these really do invite continual innovation. Obviously, their use (and the investment in them) is not limited to worship. They may be used in day care centers, schools and offices during the rest of the week.

Even when parishes successfully create a variety of liturgical communities, there is still the need for the occasional parish-wide celebration, even if it needs to be held somewhere other than the church (perhaps outdoors) to accommodate all the people. This may be at the time of a great feast like Christmas, but since the desire is to have one great liturgy for everyone, it is probably best put on an occasion when people do not have so many other plans, perhaps on a Sunday that marks the birthday of the parish or the feast of its patron. This liturgy can be planned by representatives of all the groups and should offer the best of each.

A central purpose of any program of creating communities within the parish is making the local group important to the parishioner. The local group becomes the primary realization of the church that Rahner spoke of. It is through such a group that the church exists and in such a group that persons adhere to the church.

Limited size is absolutely essential to creating this kind of a feeling for the church. Liturgy becomes the gathering point because it is through common prayer that the church group touches most completely and most deeply on those things which they share. This is not to say that members do not feel comfortable in another group, another city, another land; hospitality must become one of the marks of any worship group. But one's own group remains the place where, with others one has come to know, there is shared work in the creation of ritual and a knowledge that here are others who find in these kinds of signs the greatest possible expression of their faith, as well as a means for the growth and communication of that faith.

3.
**The
eventful
language
of
liturgy**

Normally most of the effort in the planning of a Sunday eucharist will go toward the liturgy of the word for it is here primarily that the theme will be developed. The first step, of course, is the selection of such a theme. With the proper preparation, homework, of the planning group, this business of theme selection should not occupy a great deal of time. On most occasions, then, with many of the parts of the celebration set by long-range decisions (e.g., what common parts are sung, whether or not the Gloria and Creed are recited every Sunday), the planners can assign those tasks that need to be done in light of the theme (writing the prayer of the faithful, for example); decide on appropriate music for entrance, communion and recessions; discuss any special visual preparation that will be needed for the service as a whole; and finally plan the liturgy of the word and any other elements for which particular preparation must be made for this theme.

The work of liturgy planners is primarily the fashioning of good ritual: they are sign-makers. They should be people who have a feel for their art but in any parish there are very many who do, so that there may be a turnover of planners as often as seems proper. They need not be the same people as those who will lead the celebration (celebrant, readers, ushers, song leader, choir, assistant ministers, other artists), for the two kinds of work call for quite different gifts.

The planners need, among them, a sense of the timing and rhythm of good celebration, knowledge of the possibilities and the resources (people, artists of various kinds, physical resources, financial ones too) at their disposal, a concern for discovering the content or theology of every theme, a feel for the people for whom they are doing the planning work, and, as much or more than anything else, imagination.

In this chapter we will be probing what this liturgical sign making is all about, what its nature and purpose is, how it relates to the notion of community. What is said of signs and their creation applies to the celebration as a whole and to all the parts, those common to each Sunday as well as those created to express a given theme.

Both planners and leaders of the liturgy can perform their services better if they are aware of what goes into sign-making. Our discussion will center mainly on language, since that will continue to be the predominate art form used in liturgy, but most of what is said will be true of the other art forms which hopefully will become more and more the means of worship.

We may begin with an example. In the musical version of Cervantes' *Don Quixote, Man of La Mancha,* the knight-errant encounters the local whore, Aldonza, at the inn or, for him, the castle. He calls her his lady and calls her by the name he has envisioned for such an ideal, Dulcinea. Aldonza is alternately amused and enchanted by the old man, but is brought back to reality and scorns him as her greatest tormentor for he has, by showing what might have been, made what is even more painful. But it does not end there. As the hero lies dying Aldonza and Sancho arrive. She is challenged by someone for wanting to go to the old man's side. The people there call her Aldonza. "My name," she says, "is Dulcinea."

For most people, what happens here rings true. We can say yes to it: that's the way things are. Obviously, it was not just a sound which changed Aldonza to Dulcinea, it was the faith and vision of another person. But was the word used then merely an unimportant tool? Experience says no. The word was everything. What happened could have taken place without that word only if some other experience could have been structured to do the things that word did. The word was a sign that gave Aldonza opening to a new world. It communicated more than another's thought, as words ordinarily do; it threw down a different vision of reality and challenged her to embrace it. If words may be used to do this, how are we to explain them?

Biblical scholars have been saying for a long time that the spoken word had a very different meaning for the ancients than it does for us. People may tend to think of the identification of word and action as one more prescientific quirk, happily ended now. But was it progress to move, as western man did, to a concept of language which makes it strictly subservient to "meaning" and gives it a relatively unimportant place in any hierarchy of human values? Perhaps it is we who are poorer for losing the sense of the word's power, emptying it, degrading it to another commodity.

Experiences like that in *Man of la Mancha* and even our everyday experience of words proves that the power is still there.

Whoever speaks, therefore, not only employs an expressive symbol but goes forth out of himself, and the word that he lets fall decides the matter. Even if I merely say "Good Morning" to someone I must emerge from my isolation, place myself before him and allow some proportion of my potency to pass over into his life, for good or evil. . . . The word, then, is a decisive factor: whoever utters words sets power in motion. (G. van der Leeuw, *Religion: Its Essence and Manifestation,* pp. 403-405.)

For an understanding of the use of words (and other signs too) in liturgy, we need an approach to them which takes into account their power. One such approach has been developed by philosophers like Remy Kwant. (See his *The Phenomenology of Language.*) Kwant considers words as a way of "pointing." When we physically point at someone, by a nod or with our hand, we give that person a meaning which does not exist apart from our pointing: "pointing makes something happen, but the sphere in which this happening occurs is not unqualifiedly the sphere of physical reality."

A cripple cannot hide his infirmity; he cannot prevent others from seeing his deformity. Yet he can demand that others do not point to his deformity or speak about it in his presence. If they do it anyhow, his deformity begins to exist in a new and more striking way both for himself and for others. Pointing raises a meaning out of its relative concealment. (Kwant, p. 62.)

Speaking is a way of pointing which allows us to transcend temporal and physical limitations. It allows us to bring a meaning to the foreground, to set this meaning off somewhat from its source. By speaking, persons, through a process of detaching and connecting meanings, meaning that they know through living, give these a new way of existing. The whole assembly of these words of ours constitutes "the world-for-us, the

only world about which we are able to speak," and the
world in which we are able to move most freely and be
most ourselves.

Thus a community of people is constituted by a
shared field of understood meanings, or significations,
their common speech. This insight makes some contemporary phenomena understandable: long-held worlds
are challenged and begin to come apart, threatening
those who cannot open up to a new world. For example, the whole group of significations that surrounded
the term "girl" (any woman who did secreterial work
or cleaning), or the common presumption that certain
titles go only with men ("Dr." "Judge" "Umpire"
"President") or the whole set of associations with the
terms "housewife" and "homemaker." When a different vision is brought to speech in terms like "Ms."
"God, our mother," or "After concluding her homily,
the celebrant. . . ." the old universe of discourse is
shattered, or placed on the defensive. Each must decide
how to deal with the threat to the old and, out of these
decisions, come new communities where enough is
shared to make one comfortable.

There is a process at work here which everyone has
experienced in today's quickly changing times. The accepted way of speaking is not accepted for long. There
come constant challenges and renewals. Kwant distinguishes the "spoken word" from the "speaking word."
The former is our everyday speech, but the latter is creative, it is what first gives rise to meaning and significa-
tion. "It makes use, of course, of available words, but it
makes them say something which they had never said
before." (p.143)

At the march on Washington in August of 1963,

Martin Luther King, Jr., said, "I have a dream." The words have become a part of our vocabulary, but can never mean again what they meant that day. Four ordinary words brought a vision to expression, a vision the hearer could not miss and was forced to decide about. This is the "speaking word." It is this that is behind the "spoken word"—the editorials, the laws, the court decisions, the sermons. And when the latter become exhausted, then the "speaking word" must again be heard if the vision is to remain alive.

Kwant says of the one who utters the "speaking word":

When he succeeds in increasing this light and expressing it in words, then it is as if the others were waiting for this increased enlightenment. They recognize themselves in his new way of speaking. (p. 147)

The reality that King gave word to simply would not have been real in the same way for those who have heard had he not spoken as he did. Thus the word attains an unsurpassed importance in human community, being entirely dependent on that community while at the same time the community lives by it and is entirely dependent upon it both in the "speaking" and the "spoken" forms.

Our language is an order that we impose upon all reality; most of us are open to reordering at least parts of our common universe, but only a few are able to give voice to the new words that need to be said. Around the "speaking word" a community is gathered of persons who can say "Amen" to that word. That word constitutes them a community by giving them something to share. But the word does not come from outside, it is itself the product of the community: for King to have spoken as he did, there had to be a readiness that was the work of the whole assembly of those ready to live within his word.

Speaking gains much of its meaning and its power from silence, from listening. The poet deserves attention, the word deserves quiet thought. Otherwise the order that language, especially new language, proposes for our world cannot be received. Bonhoeffer, from prison, called for the religious community to be silent, for its traditional language had become powerless. Christian thought, speech and organization had to be reborn from silent action and prayer. But he believed in a new day: "The day will come when men will be called again to utter the word of God with such power as will change and renew the world." (*Letters and Papers from Prison,* Macmillan, 1962, p. 187.)

Contemporary theologians have used concepts like these in speaking of what happened in the preaching of Jesus. Various terms like "language event" and "word event" are used to describe the situation when language throws the listener into confusion and demands change or decision. Jesus opened to his hearers a new universe of discourse, a bold alternative to that of the times, and invited them to share in it. From everyone who understood, there had to be a decision for or against. With this new language a community was created.

Language is eventful. Not all language, of course, partakes of this character. Much day-to-day business of living depends on a language which merely communicates information. But language as event is a happening of the deepest human dimensions. An illustration:

The other person is not simply called a brother because he is; he would not be a brother, if I did not so call him. Through my calling him brother I certainly do not make him into one, but I admit him as a brother among us by myself entering into community with him. (Ernst Fuchs, *Studies of the Historical Jesus*, p. 209.)

Jesus' use of the word "Father" is this kind of event. It places man in a new situation and defines that situation, and the hearer cannot do otherwise than decide if this is to be his or her existence; if it is, that person may enter into the new community. Now the community of those who accept the word of Jesus must continue to speak that word (which means they must continue to hear it) in such a way that it continues to be eventful for themselves and for others in exactly the same way it was when Jesus first spoke it and when the community first heard it.

At this point, it may be helpful for you to make this practical by calling to mind times when you have encountered what we have been calling the "speaking word." What words, or other signs, have, in great or small ways, thrown one set of assumptions, on which you were basing your life, up against another with such force that you had to make a decision?

One such event in my own experience occurred within a liturgical context. It was the first time I witnessed dance within a worship service and I was predisposed not to like it. But I was overwhelmed immediately by the power and beauty of what the dancers did. It was not simply a question of being opened up to a manner of worship I had been previously unwilling to accept, though that was one change. The other was in the

content of the dance itself, which would have been
equally strong had the dance medium posed no problem
in itself. The dance went with the religious folksong,
"They cast their nets in Galilee." The first two verses
describe the quiet, everydayness of the fishermen's lives
before meeting Jesus and "the peace of God that filled
their hearts brimful, and broke them too." The third
verse:

Young John who trimmed the flapping sail
Homeless in Patmos died,
Peter who hauled the teeming net
Headdown was crucified.

I cannot remember what motions they used to describe the death of John, but during the last two lines
above, one of the dancers locked his legs around the
neck of another and hung, headdown, arms extended.
For all the words I had probably heard before about
how the fisherman Peter became the great apostle, this
was the first time it came alive for me: the simple
goodness of everyday life in Galilee as it might have
been lived to the death, instead disrupted by Jesus, and
this man Peter dying not in his village, but countries
and seas and worlds away, upsidedown on a cross because he would not consider himself worthy to die as
Jesus had. "The peace of God it is no peace . . ." the
last verse begins and that dance, those gestures, opened
up for me a new dimension in this community.

But the examples need not be from the realm of
liturgy or religion. Taken from any realm, they bring us
closer to learning what the ritual use of signs is all
about. It also becomes increasingly clear that communities centered on such signs are not "the more we get

together the happier we'll be" communities, but sharers of a certain universe of discourse, people who have accepted a common vision.

There are many ways in which that vision is understood, and that is part of the reason that we are broken into many churches. But it would be this way in any case, for the ability to celebrate the liturgy well, effectively, in a consistent manner means that we must depend on those groupings which are natural, which offer other roots for common understandings apart from faith, which allow for friendship and shared tasks. As we saw in the last chapter, we are to think of the local community as the event of the church, a simple manifestation of the human situation. To such a community ritual happens, the "speaking word" happens—out of the word of the Spirit and the creativity of the community itself.

This is the kind of task that is set before those who would plan liturgies.

Even within the security of those parts of the liturgy which do not change from week to week (and there should always be these), the effective celebration of the ritual should be done so well that it recreates the community in their shared world. But this is not one world beside many, but the world that demands it be set over against all others if it is to be the home of the believer.

Christians do not celebrate and live in a religious world as they do in a social, geographical, political, family world. The gospel they share changes the perception of all worlds. If we have been unable to create communities perhaps it is because we have given ourselves no strong signs to gather around, decide about, none that break down all our resistance to the gospel of simplicity, sharing, peace, and give us the strength to live together in this gospel world. This is the kind of creativity that liturgy planners and leaders must have: to discover and perform the signs and rituals that confront and embrace us.

It is always tempting to think that there are no new ways of celebrating the gospel, no new insights into ways of doing the eucharist. Any discouraged liturgy committee should treat itself to the musical *Godspell* at the earliest opportunity. You will hear and see the gospel preached as if it had never been preached before and, perhaps, you will see it create a community within the theater.

Pay special attention to the Last Supper sequence if you think you cannot be moved by the story we hear at every single eucharist (and especially if you think we don't need to keep the sacrifice aspect of the eucharist more in mind). The music here is in the background only, and I believe the scene would be equally strong without it. (It is from Psalm 137: By the rivers of Babylon . . .) Jesus' friends are sitting in a circle. He goes from one to another with a mirror. Each looks in it, then takes from the last one to look a cloth and begins to wipe all the make-up away.

In the following sequence all are in the same position, Jesus blesses the bread with the Hebrew blessing ("Blessed be thou, Lord our God, king of the universe, who hast given us bread from the earth") and then the cup and gives these to his friends. As the Babylon song is played, each person seems to turn inward, frozen in position. Jesus goes from one to another. Each is happy to see him (it is all in pantomime, no words are spoken), and they greet each other with a gesture that we have come to associate with that character in earlier sequences; then each realizes that this is the last moment with Jesus. The gesture of farewell is different with each one, then each returns to the frozen position.

I am not worried about finding ways of distinguishing this drama from the ritual of a Christian community (during the intermission the cast invites the audience to the stage to share wine). Though few communities could or should attempt to do just this, that experience, except for paying admission, was of the kind we have to come to expect from ritual. That is not to say that every liturgy has to be a major production, but that's the thing about *Godspell,* it wasn't a major production either.

4. Ritual and community

In religion, generally considered, what has been the function of liturgy or ritual in relation to the establishment of community? Sociologist Joachim Wach, after surveying the way natural groups (based on race, tribe, ethnic character, etc.) relate to religion, concludes that their strong cohesion is a result of an almost perfect blend of the social and religious factors. There is a process at work by which all social functions which integrate the group assume a religious meaning: "From here it is natural to engage in acts of worship as the deepest and most effective way of strengthening the existing bonds." (*Sociology of Religion,* U. of Illinois Press, 1944, p. 107.) Does this have any meaning where a specifically religious group has a membership which crosses the lines of natural groups and/or exists where there are no natural groups?

Here, Wach speaks of the "founded religions" and distinguishes three periods: the circle of disciples, the brotherhood, and the ecclesiastical body. In the first, the group immediately associated with the founder, "the life of the new group is integrated from the start by simple rites and religious practices (meditation, prayer, singing, exhortations)" (p. 137). These rites may be taken over from existing forms in the established religion and given a new interpretation (as the religious meal of the Jews was by the followers of Jesus), or they may be newly created. Whatever the case, the symbols give expression to the solidarity of the group.

The next stage, the brotherhood, where there is

still an emphasis on charismatic leadership, sees the development of cult along with doctrine and organization. The spirit still breathes freely, but the need for structures makes itself felt in every area. Wach argues that it is still cult, in spite of the development of doctrine, which unites and integrates the brotherhood. Reform groups that come in the third stage frequently aim at restoring the church to this brotherhood model; as far as cult goes, this would mean a restoration of its primacy as a uniting factor, while returning also to its simplicity and accessibility to all members.

In the third stage, that of the ecclesiastical body, forms of worship are standardized and deviation becomes suspect. The growth of the cult requires an elaborate differentiation of functions and functionaries. There is great development in the doctrinal area and in rules of conduct. Ritual now has a less vital role in integrating the life of the local church group.

In Catholicism, that ritual which played an important part for many centuries was not understood or participated in by the community. Its importance came because it was the object of the most important and familiar doctrines and rules for the faithful, and because it often offered emotional outlets, and not because it played a role even remotely comparable to that of the cult in the brotherhood. With increased objectification of dogma and ethic, as well as the standardization of cult, worship no longer serves to promote group solidarity. Liturgy in this stage has little to do with one's sense of identity with the group, though attendance at liturgy may be extremely important.

What then is possible? François Houtart speaks of the feeling of belonging as one of the functions of the church as a society. ("Sociological Aspect of the Liturgy," *Worship*, June-July 1968, p. 350ff.) Since today liturgy is not the act of a preexisting natural community, it has the potential of doing actually what it has always done theologically: constituting a specific community of Christians. To do this, liturgy will have to adapt the proper forms for communication.

To begin this, Houtart distinguishes three types of groups for which specific liturgical forms must be found: the small group, the assembly and the throng. When the individual's membership is mediated through the small group there can be some of the integrating force which ritual had at the brotherhood stage. This would seem to argue for the kind of structure discussed in the previous chapter: constituting smaller groups within the parish on the most natural bases possible and giving to them as much autonomy as possible while maintaining the support and correction that each can offer the others through their membership in the large assembly, expressed periodically in liturgical assemblies. Houtart would probably see that it would be desirable to carry this one step further and have the whole city gather once a year when a liturgy specifically suited to the "throng" would be celebrated.

If there is to be an effort to restore the strong community/ritual relationship, we shall have to take seriously the relation between the liturgical action and the individual's action apart from the liturgy. Hoon argues that abandoning any norms for admitting one to worship has done great damage to the liturgy.

In allowing the relation between the action of worship and the worshipper's action elsewhere to be severed, the nerve of integrity has been cut. And we can only expect it to be restored when the layman is made to understand that the action he is expected to put forth in worship is of a piece with the action he is expected to put forth elsewhere. (*Integrity of Worship,* Abingdon, 1971, p. 326.)

Among the questions which Hoon says we should be trying to answer: "What thought is given to, and what provision is made for, the exercise of discipline in the structures of congregational life? Is the constraint of baptismal vows taken once in years long past lifted up and repronounced? What moral preparation for worship must the congregation be taught to undertake? To what brother must they be directed to be reconciled and what penance must they practice? Where must the people fast and watch in order to pray, and how can fasting be redefined for today?" Any such sense of discipline would have obvious effects on the liturgy and community consciousness of the group.

We move now from sociology to theology. In scripture, it is the word of God which calls the people into existence. It is the word which in fact creates the people as a people through the whole process of hearing and free response. (See Bouyer's *Liturgical Piety,* pp. 24-25.)

The early Christians had at their disposal many Greek terms for fellowship and brotherhood from which to choose a name for their communities. But instead the term that quickly became dominant was *ecclesia,* the word which the Septuagint, the Greek translation of the Old Testament, had used for *qahal,* the liturgical assembly of the people of Israel, a word which has its roots in the meaning of "calling-up" the people. (See "The Church," *Bible Key Words,* Harper and Brothers, 1951, pp. 28-29.) Equally important, Paul and others applied the term not only to the whole body of Christians but also to the individual communities, thus giving these latter an importance which they can never lose. Theologically, the communication of the word, in language and in other signs, constitutes this specific church, creates a space, a common world.

In the earliest days of the church, some scholars argue that Christians continued to have noneucharistic liturgies even after they ceased to attend the synagogue. (C.F.D. Moule, *Worship in the New Testament,* John Knox Press, 1961, p. 62.)

It may have been at such liturgies that Christians made their charismatic contributions of prophecy and tongues and interpretation. This participation in the word was under the judgment of the community. Thus there was a space for the creative word, while the whole community, itself under the word, could preside over this creativity. There is a kind of reciprocal creativity: it is the word which convokes the assembly and indeed makes it to be assembly, but the assembly itself exercises a responsibility for bringing forth the word and for discerning what is and what is not authentic.

Hoon proposes one model that such a theology of worship might attempt today in his discussion of the relationship of liturgy, fellowship and service (the three marks of the New Testament church). He first argues that liturgy is nothing if not political since politics is today the battleground of salvation, the "place where the very meaning and destiny of human life are shaped." The planning of liturgy, which is the community obeying the summons to "come," might best be in the hands of those who have obeyed the command to "go." The form and substance of preaching, the kind of music sung, the prayers, symbols and ceremonies should be shaped by those engaged in the congregation's mission to the world.

Indeed, cannot the service itself be redesigned to include preparation in the form of discussion of vital social and political questions in light of the Bible, perhaps by discussion task forces organized in advance, and then to include reports from these? For that matter, the 'reporting' itself of members' experiences of ministry could constitute part of the materials of worship, perhaps tape recordings, the reading of important newspaper and magazine articles, statements of concern, and announcements and interpretations of significant events. When these acts and elements are set within the context of Bible, song, prayer, sacrament, worship may become changed into a kind of holy town meeting and take on a vitality that comes in no other way. The people can unaffectedly express their secularized consciousness and need not feel embarrassed in doing so. Similarly they can find themselves apprehended at points in their life they know to be important and hence feel worship to speak to them with truthfulness. (*Integrity of Worship*, p. 333.)

If what Hoon is suggesting sounds too much like some of the totally structureless liturgies of recent years, his remarks must be seen in the context of his whole work where the importance of structure and especially of the gospel itself are dominant themes.

The place where most of our parishes and smaller groups can most easily begin their creative work is in the homily. Even in situations where no rubric may be violated in the search for good liturgy, planners can concentrate on the quality of all that cannot be changed, as well as good variety in those parts which can be, and can exercise their creativity on the homily (providing, of course, that the clergy see their way clear). This part of the liturgy is already understood to be the creative (occasionally) work of a member of the assembly and it is relatively easy to build on this notion. Obviously, the homily is to be understood as an integral part of the whole liturgy and never as a kind of interlude.

In a 1964 essay entitled "Priest and Poet" (in *The Word: Readings in Theology,* Kennedy, 1964), Karl Rahner, though working in the context of a homily as an entirely verbal work of a priest, voiced the theory that should guide the efforts of liturgy planners. The word, Rahner says, is more than the thought, it is gift; it can bring to life and put to death. He says there are the merely useful words and there are the great words, a distinction much like that made earlier between "spoken word" and "speaking word."

The great words effect what they signify. They are not simply representations of something, they make it present. The poet is one who utters the great words so that they enter into the worlds of others. This kind of word alone can make God present for man. But this kind of word is spoken only by the poet, and this is what the preacher is called to be: not an interpreter, commentator or exegete, but a speaker of that kind of language, which, like all good signs, comes simply and directly to the whole person of the listener. Rahner is talking about making the liturgy the kind of language-event mentioned above. How is this to be done? Only in full awareness of how communication takes place in the world today, of the kind of "poems" persons today can hear.

To some, this has meant extensive efforts to use media, efforts which can also be quite costly. In the hands of competent persons, if the costs can be justified, the use of video and audio tape, rented or purchased or community-made films, multi-media presentations and similar events can be an extremely effective proclamation of the word. But if done poorly or with little understanding of the tools or the gospel itself, such methods can be disastrous. They can also be overdone. The argument can be made that persons are so saturated with T.V. and other media, that the contrast of the simple but well-spoken word can be the precise event it is meant to be. However, the skills of preaching, like those of celebrating generally, are only beginning to be awakened.

The best course may be for liturgy planners to go forward on both fronts, and perhaps a few others as well. If there is a short film that they feel will be the sign that is needed in a particular liturgy, and if that film can be smoothly and quietly run and clearly projected so that everyone in the room can see, then let it be used.

There should be a minimum of efforts to explain why such-and-such a thing was done. Let it speak for itself. There are now available a number of packages of slides which can be used with given or locally prepared spoken or musical material. Through these, planners may come to feel enough at home in the medium to do their own work. (Paulist Press publishes a series entitled *Let Us Pray* which contains slides, a tape and other participation materials on specific themes. New Life Films, Box 2008, Kansas City, Kansas 66110 also publishes a number of packages of slides and thematic meditations.)

But the verbal preaching should be developing also. The homily should never be a time for conveying announcements of any kind, nor for such things as saying hello to a new congregation or good-bye to an old one. It is in all cases to aim for eventfulness in relation to the whole of the liturgy of the word.

The planning committee must be critic also, helping to develop homilies that preach well to the particular group both in terms of idiom and content and assuring that the homily does not come across as the speech of one in power to one out but that it is fully consistent with the egalitarian essence of the Christian community. Likewise, insofar as it can, the planning group insists that the homily be rooted in the scriptures and remain faithful to them. Fidelity to the text, to the scripture, assures that the event of preaching shapes a specific kind of people and none other. This does not mean that the homily merely interprets the scripture; it may, in fact, seldom or never make a direct reference. Integrity with the scripture does not depend on that, but on attempting to let the preaching be for these hearers what the words of Jesus and the prophets were for those who heard them. Gibson Winter says that calling the biblical events holy "affirms that they are the paradigmatic events in which the ultimate meaning of our contemporary existence is disclosed." (*The New Creation as Metropolic,* Macmillan, 1963, p. 79.) That is why "unless preaching presses for some kind of human verdict and results in some kind of change, whether in the secret chamber of a man's soul or ethically in his worldly life, the Word in its fullness has not been served." (Hoon, *Integrity of Worship,* p. 167.)

Even a liturgy which is extremely well prepared stands to lose much if the homilist has not worked with the planners so that both the form and content of the homily are well integrated into the service.

Neither preacher nor planners should assume that the homily is the business of the former. It is not a matter of having a committee write a homily, but of coordination between parts of the liturgy and a willingness on all sides to understand their responsibilities to one another. The homily will ordinarily still be the work of one person. The planners should feel also that they are free to offer suggestions and criticisms afterward that will be helpful for future liturgies. These should take delivery as well as content into account.

Within the framework of spoken words, the homily can still make use of a variety of forms, perhaps hitting on one or another that seems particularly well-suited to a particular assembly. Dialogue sermons have encountered their problems, but a good leader can make them successful with the right-sized group. Lay preaching and group preaching have yet to be tried in the ordinary parish. Perhaps in some places the growth of pentecostalism within the traditions (and the openness of the tradition to its pentecostal members) will offer a point for beginning here, but preaching by lay persons in the congregation or the sharing of the homily among the laity and clergy should not wait for this.

The homily, as opportunity to address this specific group with the interpretation of the word of scripture in such a way that it becomes an event, need not be limited to the use of spoken words or electronic media. These things may be accomplished through other forms, other languages, where different kinds of talents are involved in the task of making those signs which gather and strengthen the community. Ordinarily, these will be limited more to those groups within the parish that want them: if the liturgies are of various kinds (in form, not content), then one means of distinguishing the forms and so dividing the total parish should be by the kind of preaching that will be done.

Other forms might include the dance, mime, puppetry, conventional and modern forms of drama, storytelling, music, poetry. We have discussed in the first chapter how it is with the same tools as art that ritual functions. Both are involved in making signs because only through signs is the whole of the person addressed and embraced. Because we have relied so heavily on the artistry of words, we are hesitant about other arts. We apply to them tests we would not think of applying to the form and content of the words used in liturgy. This testing is proper, but the words must subject themselves to it also, and we must constantly be careful that it is the norm of Christian liturgy that is the standard. Much time can be lost, however, unless liturgy planners are ready to plunge in and take some risks.

Because we are not accustomed to working with artists in the creation of liturgy, it will be better to err on the side of respect for their understanding of the task than to try to do their work for them. Likewise, the church should err in generosity rather than expect that the artist is able to contribute time (which, for such a person, is money even more than for the rest of us). It should not be presumed that if the artist is a member of the congregation no honorarium is necessary. Liturgy planners need to feel their way carefully here and realize that in the American way of doing things, paying for the use of talent will often insure the greatest effort and will establish a mutual respect between artist and planners.

Hoon says rightly that "art stands in relation to Christian worship as an adjective, not as a noun." (p. 273) This is the limitation on the artist. The whole of ritual is art form, but in every instance we must be concerned not only that the art is done as well as is possible, but that it is the servant of the gospel of Jesus.

Art forms are the stuff of every gospel that is preached; sometimes they are done well, sometimes not. Doing them well does not guarantee that it is the gospel of Jesus we are preaching. That is the responsibility of artist and planning committee working together. Further, liturgical art is communal: "Its language is to constitute a *koinonia* (fellowship) language suitable for the believing community—the Church." (Hoon, p. 274.) Here the artist must be first aware not of personal satisfaction but of effect on others: artist and creation are servants of the community. (All this is true no less of the traditional preacher.)

Planners need to keep a "live" and growing list of the artistic talent available in the area (not only in the immediate worshipping community). Members of the group need to explore the resources of universities, theater groups, entertainers, music groups. The graphic artists (any kind of visual creativity) should be a part of such a listing of resources and it is possible that on occasion these could also be of use in the specific context of nonverbal preaching being discussed here, though ordinarily these arts serve in the creation of the environment for worship. It is not a matter of deciding exactly what is to be done and then calling in the artist to instruct. The committee may have definite suggestions, but should remain open to the input of the artist. The latter will almost always be glad for the planners' initial guidance and continued criticism as the creation takes shape.

Obviously, the amount of groundwork that will have to be done before the introduction of new art forms into the liturgy will vary greatly from place to place. It will hardly ever be attempted until the planners have made strong efforts with the more ordinary aspects of the liturgy: the singing, environment, style of the ministers, flow of the celebration itself. This itself is a learning process for the whole congregation. When it is underway, the introduction of dance or drama will not seem that unusual.

Planners will ordinarily find it helpful, here as in other areas, to make basic commitments to try new programs for a certain amount of time. Otherwise, there is a feeling of "we'll do this once and if it doesn't work (i.e., goes over badly, meets with resistance or indifference), we won't try it again." Much better to say that for the next six months we will attempt to offer something other than the usual form of the homily at least once a month. Then, over the whole time, careful attention can be paid to the reaction. But only at the end is a decision made about how to continue.

Liturgy planners unaccustomed to thinking about the use of the arts in worship, and artists equally new to this, may have to spend some time getting to know each other, sharing ideas and insights, brainstorming. The committee especially should feel obliged to broaden its own horizons through learning: attending various kinds of artistic presentations, reading, listening to tapes and records. The advantage of having persons well versed in these areas on the committee should be obvious.

Often the first attempts at preaching through these forms will involve materials which are easily accepted by people: a scene from a drama already recognized as religious such as *Murder in the Cathedral,* a dance to the music of Handel's *Messiah,* the telling of a story such as "Saint Francis and the Wolf," a "speech choir" doing selections from the poems of Gerard Manley Hopkins, musicians and singers doing a selection from *Jesus Christ Superstar.* Thus begun, it will be easier to see how the liturgy can include the same artists doing a scene from Eugene O'Neill, a dance to a Cat Stevens' piece, a story from Greek mythology, poems from Ogden Nash, or music from James Taylor. It should be obvious from what was said above that not everything is compatible with liturgy, that in the context of specific celebration appropriateness will be determined, and that there must be consideration of what immediately precedes and follows the work of the artist.

All of the artistic contributions we have mentioned and more can be of service throughout the eucharistic liturgy and not simply as a homily. This is a beginning point that will serve well, perhaps, even in cases where there is a greater feeling of freedom to introduce visuals (slides or other) with the prayer of the faithful, dance as a meditation between readings of scripture or drama as a substitute for one of the assigned readings.

In whatever context, there should be opportunities for the use of the arts to involve the people actively at times. When the physical setting makes it possible, gesture and movement (with or without singing) should be taught to the congregation as naturally, if not as often, as song is taught. This may be limited to a few gestures with the hands and arms, or to turning in place, because of the restrictions pews place on movement.

We need to move beyond genuflections and signs of the cross (while we learn to do these with grace). In a drama or the telling of a story, there can often be a part for the congregation; this need not even be words—it can be sound effects. In the same way, the creation of the environment for worship can be placed under the direction of the artist but can involve as many as are willing to stay late or come early.

Since the freedom to use these many different forms in liturgy is felt more strongly in noneucharistic liturgies these should always include a maximum use of such experimentation. Since the group will ordinarily be smaller, the liturgy can be planned for greater involvement. It is so easy when planning a noneucharistic liturgy to begin by asking the same old questions: "What would be a good reading?" "What's a good song for this?" Those may well be necessary questions, but they aren't the most helpful way to begin planning a celebration. Try instead to get in mind three or four elements that could well be a part of this liturgy: a kind of circle dance, the quiet listening to a specific piece of music, a story that someone tells very well, an object that seems to say perfectly what needs saying (a seed, a bit of salt, ashes, whatever fits). Then comes the creation of a structure whose rhythm is vital to good liturgy. Finally, the question of when in that structure we need to sing and what song it should be. That part we can do more easily.

Communities may wish to create and use noneu-

charistic rituals which demand less special work each
time and can be repeated often with simple changes of
particular elements. Thus the community could adopt a
form of morning or evening prayer. But even here, care
needs to be taken lest the entirely verbal swallow us up.
Bodily position, gestures, silences, poetry, recorded
music and other elements can be a regular part of such
prayer without requiring more than the work that such
a liturgy should deserve. Much of what is done will be
repeatable and can be shared with other communities
and thus becomes even more worth the effort.

Through such processes as those we have been discussing, where there will be many things that planners
will regret and decide to do differently, the ritual of a
community is created: out of the community but also
creating the community. The rites or signs that are
found are those that clarify the homeground of this
group, that which they share, but also that which they
are called to.

Some may feel that this kind of celebration,
this kind of sign-creating-community-as-community-
creates-signs, is too contrived, too unnatural. Certainly,
that can at times be the effect. But the process is as natural as the creation of any rite ever was. The problem is
with the immediate tradition which has made us strang-
ers to sign making and uneasy with many of the tools
involved, including our own bodies. We have little
background for saying that something is contrived or
not natural because it does not fit comfortably with
what we have known as liturgy.

In this final chapter we want to look more closely at the *what* of liturgy, though this can never be fully separated from the *how* which we have been looking at as the question of forms.

We have spoken of the eventfulness of good ritual as the characteristic which makes it live within a given assembly, making community possible. We want to study here one area that may illustrate the whole process of how signs (words and others) embody a content and create a specific community. We will be discussing Jesus' use of parables and asking what it is that happened when Jesus spoke these.

First, we need to understand what a parable is. Unfortunately, too many still think of them as allegories; this has been the temptation since they were first written down with the commentary of the early church: "The seed is the word of God. . . ." Contemporary scholarship has shown that this was not the way they were used by Jesus. Rather, we have a group of simple, clear stories where everyone can, up to a point, easily accept the characters and the action. Parables are not illustrations of any particular point or idea, rather they transcend any particular idea and grasp a whole. (Here and throughout this section we will be drawing on the work of Robert Funk in *Language, Hermeneutic, and the Word of God,* Harper and Row, 1966.)

Parables are a kind of language that we have called above the "speaking word," that is, they are creating new ways of seeing and existing in reality. They are not explanations of old meanings, but creations of new meaning. Parables then aren't limited to one kind of listener, nor are they filled with only one set of ideas. They go at something so deep that every hearer feels a part of himself being challenged. The parable places the hearer in a new situation, opens a new kind of existence that may be chosen or rejected.

In the parable the listener is drawn into a world that is easily recognized, or so it seems: a lost piece of money, a young man squandering his wealth, the sowing of seed in springtime. By the time the listener realizes that there is also something strange here, he must decide whether to "unfold with the story . . . or reject the call and abide with the conventional." (Funk, p. 162.) The contrast of the familiar and strange, the known and the unknown comes in an element of exaggeration, or a surprise in the narrative, or a paradox, or in something more subtle.

So the listener comes into the story with the teller and must decide whether or not to abide in the situation the parable has created. Eta Linnemann says that even where the listener "persists in his previous position, it is not simply 'all as before.' " That old position has lost its character of inevitability: it has now been chosen.

So a successful parable is an event in a double sense; it creates a new possibility in the situation, and it compels the man addressed to a decision. . . . Anyone who risks a parable in such a situation is risking everything; but this is the only way he can win everything. (Eta Linnemann, *Jesus of the Parables,* Harper and Row, 1966, pp. 30-31.)

The situation which the parables of Jesus convey to the hearer is so at variance with their own understanding of themselves and their world, that the risk is

great indeed. The parable thus threatens those who remain in their old world precisely because they now
know it is not the only one and that there are others
who have chosen this new world. So essential is this
choice, and so obvious to both sides, that the parables
and the cross are directly related.

A direct line leads from the parables of Jesus to his
crucifixion. . . . May one not say that by his parables
he put his life at stake, that he risked his life for the
word that could bring his listeners into agreement with
him, that made possible for them this change of existence, this faith? (Linnemann, pp. 40-41.)

We know what it means to say that one interprets
a poem, or a parable. What we are talking about here is
what happens when one is interpreted by the parable.
That is the event. That is the point at which we pass
beyond discursive use of language and encounter the
"speaking word." How does this "being interpreted"
happen? The parables are normally said before both
Jesus' opponents and those considered sinners. For example, as the parable of the prodigal son unfolds, each
listener identifies himself.

The auditors are now invited to consider their response;
they either rejoice because as sinners they are glad to be
dependent on grace, or they are offended because they
want justice on top of grace. They cannot go away and
come back another day to give their decision. . . .
When man has been addressed by the word of grace, he
has already been interpreted. (Funk, p. 16.)

To those who become Jesus' opponents, there is
something terribly wrong with a God who lavishes
grace in a word, who "turns the righteousness (not hy-

pocrisy!) of the Pharisee out . . ."

The Pharisees are those who insist on interpreting the word of grace rather than letting themselves be interpreted by it. (Funk, p. 17.)

But for sinners who can hear the word of grace with joy, there is a new kind of life. Thus the parable becomes decisive for all who listen, and there is no in between.

An important aspect in this understanding of the parables is the fact that Jesus too becomes one who hears the parable. He gives the parable "a certain measure of independence over against himself and, in so doing, moves to the side of his auditors vis-a-vis the parable." (Funk, p. 17.) The speaker of the parable is not above it: he too must respond to the parable, must allow his own existence to be interpreted by it and decide to live in the world which it has brought to meaning. Jesus does not identify with any group as such, but will be with those who hear the word and rejoice. The decision is theirs as it is his. They know he has made his decision and will be there with them should they follow. His dining with sinners is one way his own decision about the prodigal son situation is expressed.

To say that Jesus is also hearer means that what happens when he says a parable resembles the event of so many western films: the leader of the besieged fort draws a line in the dirt and invites all who will fight to the death to step over; he draws himself into this "fight and die" side.

It is Jesus' own conduct which demonstrates that the parables are not simply a call to sinful man to believe in God's kindness. They contain pledge and determination on the part of Jesus: pledge that those who hope in God will not be disappointed, and determination to give all for this faith. "The proof of the parable was finally revealed only on the cross." (Ernst Fuchs, *Studies of the Historical Jesus,* SCM Press, 1964, p. 37.) Jesus believed the word which he spoke. We have seen that this word in the parable of the prodigal son is a word of God's love, and God's love becomes event through the word.

Whoever receives the *verdict* of love through its promise—and this is proclaimed only to the beloved—has reason to rejoice. For love sets free. It is greater than we. (Fuchs, p. 161.)

In the parables Jesus shared the freedom he himself has found, freedom that is for others, freedom that leads to the cross. This freedom was indescribable in the bounds of logical language and could only fully break through in the parables as eventful language; there it presented itself as a vision of man's situation before God which could be accepted with joy or rejected with anger.

The actions and parables of Jesus make God's kindness present; knowledge of God becomes possible in the joyous reception of Jesus' word. What kindness bestows is freedom, "not just on the person concerned, but on every understanding community." (Fuchs, p. 155.) Those who understand what the story of the laborers in the vineyard is all about and accept it as their own situation are set free, and they share among themselves this common knowledge of God. Jesus revealed his own decision regarding man's situation before God and other men by "gathering together the unorganized group of the eschatological community in the midst of a perverse generation." (Fuchs, p. 24.)

What this community has is not simply a togetherness but a shared vision of reality that does not bind them together so much because it is at odds with that of the majority in the society as because a vital part of this new vision is a gracious acceptance of one another even as man has found gracious acceptance with God.

Robert Funk, whom we have quoted above, offers an example of the parable as event with the parable of the great supper. He stresses the parable's aspects of everydayness (a man gives a dinner and sends out invitations) and of strangeness (every single one of them refuses, the man fills the hall with a multitude of the lower classes). The meal itself takes on a "never-never land" quality that is climaxed when the original guests show up and have the doors closed in their faces. And that is all. There is no conclusion. (Funk, pp. 176-191.)

What does the parable say? Funk answers with reference to Jesus' audience. The well-off like the idea of a banquet, don't like the idea that the story makes people like them refuse to come: at least they want to know more about it—there must be some special circumstances. The poor, on the other hand, would never expect to be included in a story about a great banquet. All run ahead to the outcome, though the destiny toward which they severally rush is shattered in the narrative: "neither group is able to negotiate the abrupt corners." And there is no conclusion. The parable ends. And everyone knows where he stands. (Funk, pp. 191-193.)

The parable allows for each listener to relate individually to the story.

As the story unfolds, he must make up his mind whether he can unfold with it, i.e., whether he is congenial to its development. If, as the story reaches its turning point, this one or that one draws back, we know who he is! If, as the story comes to its climax, we see a smile pass these lips or those, we have identified him, too! (Funk, p. 192.)

Nothing at all has been presupposed. Each listener is taken by surprise since the story does not deal as expected with the matter at hand. The parable then is really talking about something apart from the subject under consideration and thus allows a new dimension in what can be said about the subject. The outcome of the parable is in the audience.

What the parable says cannot be said any other way. To interpret a parable, a person must speak a parable. The particular parables of Jesus function in the world he knew and relate to the everydayness of the people he met. The grace they offer is attested only by their own eventfulness. A true parable cannot give criteria more dependable than itself for the new world which invokes the parable.

The church has, of course, continued to use the parables of Jesus. But from the very beginning, when they were addressed to persons of different backgrounds, they took on a different meaning. What was eventful for those who listened to Jesus in Galilee could not be so for those who heard Paul in Rome. The task was not to repeat the parable, but to repeat the event of the parable in new circumstances: the language, or other signs, used by the preachers had to qualify the worlds of the hearers as Jesus' parables had qualified the worlds of his hearers, and this language had to present a new reality, one capable of bestowing on the hearer that gracious freedom which the language-event of Jesus' parables bestowed on those who heard and accepted.

Funk refers to the language of the parables as the "foundational language" of the Christian community:

If the parable is that mode of language which founds a world, and that particular world under the domain of God's grace, all other language in the Christian tradition is derivative in relation to it. It is out of this "poetic" medium that the tradition springs, however far it may subsequently wander from it. (Funk, p. 244.)

Funk argues that Christian discourse and theology must return again and again to the foundational language as test of fidelity.

Preaching repeats the *event* that happened to Jesus' listeners through the parables of Jesus. . . . Preaching, however, not only receives instructions from the parables of Jesus on how it is to be done rightly, but is grounded in what Jesus did when he risked his word. (Linnemann, p. 33.)

There is a conservative force in language which works against the language-event, seeking security in the continuing efficacy of what once happened in language and needs only to be reproduced—not as event but as formula. The working of this process is abundantly clear in the history of the church as institution, but it appears even in the early church where the parables of Jesus were often seen as allegories or simply "stories with a point."

We need not catalog our own failings here. The point is simply to grasp what the function of the parable was and what the function of liturgical signs has to be if we are to gather ourselves into the community which was first summoned by the parables of Jesus. Language (the whole realm of signs which are the elements of ritual) is not one factor among many determining the community of the faithful, but is in fact primary in the creation and definition of that people. But the community also creates the language which is to be constantly new as new human situations are confronted; its newness must be faithful to the foundation, the language which came to event in Jesus.

There are today great numbers of Christians who want the church to be the community they need; there are even more who have yet to define this need. In the last three chapters we have seen how language creates meaning for man, and among men creates a common world. This common world is shaped by man's own creative speaking. This "speaking" we may understand today not only as embracing all of the traditional art forms that are involved in making signs, but also those contemporary forms involving electronic media. (There is another side to this which we can only refer to: in this same world of technology, man may be imprisoned by language, the "speaking word" taken from him along with the ability to dissent, to criticize, to make fundamentally different choices from those offered to him by big government, big business and the other man-made regulators of life.)

The liturgy of the word, and indeed all liturgy, is meant to name a certain world of meaning and thus create a community for those who decide to share this meaning. There is today a tremendous gap between this theological understanding of the liturgy and the reality.

What is clear is that if there is to be a Christian community, it will find itself only insofar as its world is created by ritual. But that ritual is the work of the people, the liturgy (that's what the word means). From the parables of Jesus we can learn much about the "strategies and vehicles of Christian speech and then adapt these to our own situation." (Amos Wilder, *The Language of the Gospel,* Harper and Row, 1964, p. 13.) We learn content and form together. Naturally, we cannot risk less than Jesus did when we embark on speaking this language: we risk everything. The church, long on record for faithful listening to the word, is challenged now to creative speaking of the word.

People seem to be ready for this. Even more, they seem to be ready to learn from mistakes they make in the creation of liturgies. There is still far too little asked of liturgy by clergy and laity alike; each demands too little of the other, both are ordinarily far too willing to see liturgy given a fairly low priority believing, evidently, that the Christian community can be created around education, youth activities, sensitivity groups or political activity. That would be fine in some other world, but it is not the way things work here: as followers of Jesus our agenda is set, our world created, in the common ritual. That is where there happens in sign, and so most wholly, what we wish to effect through any other program. We have been quite limited in seeing the possibilities of liturgy, in taking it beyond the church building and the eucharistic format. We haven't tried to find and fashion the kinds of rituals that carry the day-to-day burdens and joys and the once-in-a-life-time burdens and joys. We have only begun to feel again the meaning and power of prayer—alone and in groups.

There is every reason why our culture resists such movements. There is a great moment in the movie *The Last Picture Show* when two friends are discussing Sam, the owner of the theater and pool room who has recently died. One is Sonny, the young boy to whom Sam left the poolhall, the other is a woman whom Sam had told the boy about once when they were fishing. She was much younger than Sam but the two of them had once spent some wild and playful hours together at the waterhole the town called a lake.

Each knows the other's love for Sam and the fantastic difference his death has made: he was the little town's only spark of imagination, humor, affection without first questioning. The woman says something like, "Thank God for Sam. Without him, I'd have never found it, whatever *it* is." As far removed as we might like to think we are from that little Texas town of the early fifties, we are pretty much the products of the same culture two or three steps further on.

The task of Christian ritual in such a culture is much like that of Sam: it presents an alternative that reveals the unfreedom of our existence and the gospel of a different way. Often for those who celebrate this ritual there is no withdrawal from the town: the dimension it adds makes so much difference that all the possibilities of the culture begin to reveal themselves. This is the liberating task that was referred to above in the discussion of Jesus and the parables. It is political, economic, social, religious. It addresses us as members of families, as consumers, as war makers and potential unleashers of genocide, as victims of our own national greed, as alienated from nearly all the ways in which man could have learned to make earth a household, as racist and as sexist, as desperately in need of finding a self. There is quite simply no other way for it to come to us. Like the woman who loved Sam, we may not be able to articulate what *it* is, but we can't help knowing when we have experienced its announcement that the kingdom of God is near to us if we will be converted.

The creation of this kind of public ritual is greatly dependent on our willingness to become again makers and users of signs in the times between the gatherings of the community. "The sense of reality felt by the congregation as it acts to pray when gathered is conditioned by the members' faithfulness to prayer when dispersed." (Hoon, p. 328.) No one knows how to face the task of living out alternatives to war, discrimination, the greed of nations like our own, the continuing rape of the earth, the ethic of consumption and competition. But the very substance of our ritual, of our prayer, is concerned with making us living alternatives to these evils. In our common prayer, at the dinner table as at the altar (and they are interdependent) we make the signs of the kingdom which we want to live in, we make rituals which in turn summon us to a space they have created.

Any serious Christian community should involve itself in taking to heart a small book by Dietrich Bonhoeffer called *Life Together* (published in this country by Harper and Row in 1954). In the first few pages he reflects on the wonder and gratitude that should fill the Christian who has the opportunity to live in community with other Christians.

So between the death of Christ and the Last Day it is only by a gracious anticipation of the last things that

Christians are privileged to live in visible fellowship with other Christians. It is by the grace of God that a congregation is permitted to gather visibly in this world to share God's Word and sacrament. (p. 18.)

Perhaps we shall one day recall our concern with community and liturgy in the parish community and be amazed that we were so slow to seek it in that visible fellowship which constitutes most of our parishes, the family. And in groups of families and people who live alone. Again, it is the culture: families are not places for taking life and death seriously. It is difficult to imagine the difference this would make.